Twelve Quakers and Pacifism

by

Quaker Quest

Quaker Quest Pamphlet 3

Also available in this series:

Twelve Quakers and God (2004)
Twelve Quakers and Worship (2004)
Twelve Quakers and Evil (2006)
Twelve Quakers and Simplicity (2006)
Twelve Quakers and Jesus (2007)
Twelve Quakers and Equality (2007)

Published in 2005 in the United Kingdom by Quaker Quest, an outreach project of Hampstead Monthly Meeting, Britain Yearly Meeting of the Religious Society of Friends (Quakers).

ISBN: 0-9543459-3-2

1st printing 2005: 2,000 copies
2nd printing 2007: 1,000 copies

Preface

Quaker Quest is a series of open meetings for people interested in the Quaker way as a spiritual path for today which is simple, radical and contemporary. The project began in London in 2002 and now Quaker Quest events are held throughout Britain.

In 2004, members of the London Quaker Quest team published two booklets, *Twelve Quakers and God* and *Twelve Quakers and Worship*. Each volume was a short collection of personal reflections on themes which stand at the heart of the Quaker faith.

Now the team has decided to publish a third in the series. The ground rules for *Twelve Quakers and Pacifism* remain the same as for the first two pamphlets - nobody has seen the others' contributions until all twelve have been completed, and the anonymity of the authors has been protected.

For some of the writers, feelings about peacemaking, pacifism and conscientious objection, so vital to many Quakers, have proved even more difficult to express in a short space than the previous topics. These are not simple matters and no one wants to pretend that they are. We hope, however, that this short collection of personal views may begin to help some who are starting to explore the Quaker way in the twenty-first century.

Introduction

"Do I have to be a pacifist to be a Quaker?"

When Quakers are asked about their faith, this question often comes first. The answer to it is a very simple one: no. There is no requirement for Quakers to be pacifists. *Quaker Faith & Practice*, our book of Christian discipline, is quite clear - "complete agreement with all our testimonies is not necessary".

Yet the peace testimony is, without question, central to the Quaker faith. It stems directly from our testimony to equality, and many newcomers to Quakerism feel strongly that they want to learn more about it. Some find that the word "pacifism" can prove to be a real stumbling block as they try to move forward. We hope that this book may be of use to them.

Quakers are not always in agreement on issues of peace. Some feel that pacifism is not necessarily part of the Quaker peace testimony at all. Many are clear that it is peace-building that we need to concentrate on, rather than a negative "no war" stance which may not be helpful.

The twelve Quakers who have written these pieces are of differing ages and backgrounds, and their views on pacifism differ too. We hope that readers will find such diversity stimulating and that this booklet may help them as they form, and perhaps change, their own opinions.

1

My abhorrence of war is very deep seated, a truly gut feeling which I have had for as long as I can remember. There are many arguments and justifications that I can put forward to support this stance, as can all pacifists. I can say that peacemaking and nonviolence are intrinsically linked to my basic Quaker belief that every person has the capacity to know and love God, and that we are all unique, precious, children of God. I can quote Biblical injunctions: thou shalt not kill; you are to love your neighbour as yourself. I can argue from history that violence only begets violence, and that no lasting peace has ever been built on violence and injustice.

But I believe that at the very root of my pacifism, and I believe of most others, is a compellingly strong feeling, not a reasoned argument but a feeling, that it is simply wrong to hurt another human being. The issue of war and violent resolution of conflict is to me a matter of black and white in an otherwise often grey world. War is wrong. Violence is wrong. Harming others is wrong. War is so heinous a crime that any nonviolent action to prevent or stop it is justified.

I am sickened when I see the country in which I live and work and pay taxes deploying its army to kill and destroy in distant lands. It is being done in my name; my tax money pays for it; I profit from the loot that is seized; I am responsible. I can no more evade my involvement than can those victims who are bombed, or shot dead while their homes are razed to the ground. They are harmed. I am responsible, and am myself harmed. We are all caught up in the jaws of war. Do not ask for whom the bells of war toll; they toll for every one of us.

As a pacifist I am often challenged on the issue of self-defence. How would I respond if I, or my family or neighbours, were to be personally attacked? I don't think this question can be answered hypothetically, as none of us can be sure what instantaneous response we might make under sudden personal attack. My reaction might well be impulsive rather than cerebral. It's possible it would be violent, but it wouldn't be premeditated violence. I remember the fierce protective instinct that possessed me when I had a baby to care for, and how I was overwhelmed by the force of my emotions and reactions at that time.

This issue, however, is surely a long way from the war preparations of nations: the calculated stockpiling of weaponry of destruction; the training of young men and women in the arts of killing; the strategic military plans awaiting implementation. It's a long way from war and the readiness for war. And I like the response of the conscientious objector in the Second World War who was challenged as to how he would respond if his sister were to be raped by "the enemy". "Well," he said, "I wouldn't want to respond by bombing the rapist's sister."

Similar to the frequently asked question of self-defence is that of disarmament. "Would you really have our nation unilaterally lay down all arms and disband all military forces?" I am asked. Of course not. Effective disarmament would have to be a gradual process, achieved in concert among the nations of the world. It would require the leadership of men and women of vision in the militarised nations. They would have to recognise their nations' self-interest in reducing economic exploitation of weaker nations and in relinquishing military strength in order to strengthen world security. It would mean re-deploying national forces into international peacekeeping forces. Its success would depend on an arms-control system based upon fairness, not upon nuclear powers strengthening their own capacities while preaching non-proliferation to others. In short, it would depend upon trust, foresight, justice and respect - in fact, upon loving one's neighbour.

I like to think that some day humanity will view the wars of the twentieth and twenty-first centuries with the abhorrence with which we now view the gladiatorial contests of ancient Rome. People will wonder how human society could ever have tolerated the pitting in deadly combat of one group of young men, and now women, from one country against a similar group from another country. It will seem to them grotesque that massive resources were poured into lethal weaponry of death, destruction and torture while large segments of humanity went hungry and while simple illnesses went untreated. It will seem to them imperative to find nonviolent solutions to the perennial conflicts in the world, and to practice pacifism.

2

Quaker belief in peace derives from a specific event in 1660 - the declaration to Charles II when Quakers were accused of seeking to overthrow the government: "our principle is, and our practices have always been, to seek peace, and ensue it". But the coming of World War in

1914 and of conscription in 1916 made the need for a living testimony to peace - and to conscientious objection - more urgent. The horrors of the First World War, and the increasing likelihood of another one during the twenties and thirties, led Dick Sheppard, vicar of St. Martin-in-the-Fields and popular as "the radio parson", to launch in 1934 the Peace Pledge Union. Its declaration was "We renounce war and never again, directly or indirectly, will we support or sanction another." Membership grew steadily. Even in September 1939, when war was again declared, 2,435 new members joined; in October another 2,280. By April 1940 membership had risen to 136,000. It was not until the fall of France in May 1940 that numbers started to drop sharply.

The treatment of conscientious objectors in the First World War - many of whom suffered in prison - led the government in its 1939 Military Training Act (which re-introduced conscription) to provide for tribunals to decide about those claiming exemption as conscientious objectors. Between 1939 and 1945, more than 67,000 did so - nearly four times as many as in the earlier war. Six per cent of these were "absolutists" who refused to perform any compulsory alternative service. Friends, led by Arnold Rowntree and Paul Cadbury, decided to form again the Friends' Ambulance Unit, which had existed in the earlier war. Three hundred applied to join in the first few days, and priority was given to Friends and those who had attended Quaker schools. Throughout the war 5,000 people enquired about membership and 1,314, including 97 women, actually joined, "spreading their humanitarian service throughout Britain and to far-flung places abroad". The unit was open to anybody who shared basic Quaker beliefs that war is inconsistent with the spirit and teaching of Jesus and that the individual should be active in the task of reconciliation between individuals, groups and nations.

Because of my age, I happened to be one of the first to appear before a "tribunal" (itself perhaps rather confused about its function) in 1939. The experience convinced me that no tribunal, nor any person, can truly decide whether another individual's reasoning and decision is conscientious or not. I was brought up in a Church of England home, but with an unusually strong pacifist background. I soon heard about the Friends Ambulance Unit and decided that I would rather work with them than do nothing or perhaps go to prison. Over five years, I found myself in the East End of London during the blitz, spending a year each in China and in India, and, after the war ended in the West, among the displaced Poles of north Germany. I am not proud of what I did during the war, but I do not regret it. Four of my friends later decided they had made a mistake and joined the forces.

Since 1945, ironically due to the atom bomb, there have been sixty years of peace between the major powers, leading dangerously to there being only one superpower. Yet wars continue, most recently in Iraq, and weapons become ever more deadly and destructive. The need for Quaker pacifism and its clear expression remains ever more urgent. Yet, though Friends sometimes seem curiously reluctant to emphasise or even discuss the peace testimony in public, pacifism is an essential and central part of Quakerism. In it, the sacred and the secular come more closely together than almost anywhere else.

For me, the Holy Spirit, the conscience and George Fox's idea of Truth are almost three expressions of the same belief, based on experience. The letters C.O. should stand for conscientious obedience - obedience to conscience - rather than conscientious objection. Each of us must follow the promptings of his or her own conscience.

3

I come from a long line of good people who never questioned the use of violence or the necessity of going to war. Maybe it was because my father died when I was four that I questioned this. I believed, from an early age, that life was something we could not restore - hence should not take. Once I went to Sunday School and discovered the Ten Commandments and Jesus' words about loving our enemies I was confirmed as an earnest five-year-old pacifist, withdrawing my support from all violence and violent structures. I recall a tinge of sadness that there was no more conscription, so I was unlikely to be a public conscientious objector!

As I grew up I realised that it wasn't (all) about passivity and withdrawal. It had to be about action to prevent things happening. So off I went on CND marches and anti-Vietnam War demos. I was troubled by so much of the violence on the edges of these and worked to try to make them more peaceful. (A wonderful toolbox of "nonviolent action" has been, and is being, built up by people all over the world and I wish I had known and understood more about this years ago.)

Then I saw that prevention wasn't (just) about protest. Nonviolence (in the peace movement this is a non-hyphenated word to emphasise its positive nature) includes building good relations between people, helping them to deal with their conflicts creatively. It must include working with those who are disadvantaged, addressing the injustices that lead to conflicts and then building the institutions locally, nationally and internationally which make for peace. That's not an idealistic, impossible agenda. Most of us are able to engage where we are as local people, in the work place and nationally when opportunity arises. Sometimes I still find myself in a situation where passive non-cooperation seems the right thing; at other times I hope I have been able to contribute to moving things forward creatively.

Quakers have never been very exercised by the hypothetical. I don't spend much time thinking "What would I do if..." I believe I act well by conscious preparation - and that includes my worship, prayer and learning about peace and nonviolence. My Quakerism helps me hold a vision in front of me of a nonviolent world. This is not easy. I never argue that nonviolence always "works" in the short term, only that I can act no other way. So it offers me a community of support, not least because it reminds me that I don't have to be active on every issue all the time. I can do what I can, where I can, as best I can and feel connected to others acting in their own way.

I have grown into an understanding that peace is not conflict free. *Life* is not conflict free. Learning how to handle conflict is one of the ways we grow to maturity. It is *how* we handle it that matters. The means must mirror the end we seek - so they must be just, healing and transforming.

Above all, I believe passionately that evil cannot be overcome by using its own methods, or by destroying the individuals involved in it. It needs to be confronted and transformed. The cycles of violence have to be stopped.

There are no exceptions. I have to live as though that is *always* true - and I cannot do that in my own strength alone.

4

I don't like the word "pacifism" very much. Could it be that my slightly negative feeling comes simply from its similarity to the word "passive"?

I haven't been a pacifist all my life. In fact, when I first started to attend Quaker meetings, I found the peace testimony quite a stumbling block. I could understand the emotional longing for an end to war, but it seemed logical to me that military force was sometimes needed in desperate circumstances.

I understand now that I was making a connection which is entirely false. I thought that if people have a just cause, any war that they wage will, more or less by definition, be a just one. In time, I learned to pull this connection apart. I began slowly to understand that, while there may be many just causes, it absolutely does not follow that there is ever such a thing as a just war.

I have been very disturbed to read how passionately this idea of the just war is defended in Christian literature. St. Augustine and St. Thomas Aquinas, for example, both argued that it is a right to use evil methods if your aim is the avoidance of evil. It's an utterly fatuous idea, but for some reason its absurdity seems to be lost on a lot of us. It was certainly lost on me.

I now look back on my old ideas with some disbelief. I find myself to be passionately opposed to all military action, for whatever reason. I'm too young to have been called up, but I am confident that had I lived through any of the wars I know about, I would have been, for religious reasons, a conscientious objector.

"The Christian ideal has not been tried and left wanting. It has been found difficult; and left untried." G.K. Chesterton wrote that in 1910, and during the hundred or so years since, nothing has changed. "Difficult" concepts (thou shalt not kill; love your enemies; do good to those who hate you) become impossible in times of war and are conveniently forgotten.

The misery suffered by people in the firing line is well documented: we all know about the indescribable horrors of armed conflict. But so long as they have what Thomas Aquinas called "a rightful intention", good people still justify the deliberate murder of others. Perhaps it's sensible to remember how rarely, if ever, those rightful intentions have been realised, how often and how subtly they are corrupted. For example, in 1939 well-intentioned, reasonable people declared war on Germany in order to liberate Poland. And in 1945 they bombed Hiroshima.

And if wars were ever proved to solve problems, what then? Well, if I base my life on my religion, I have to value that more than pure practicality. So I need to start at the other end and look at it from a religious perspective. And as soon as I do that, I discover a truth which, as far as I am concerned, cancels out everything else. It is this: nobody can take part in a war without showing contempt for the transforming power of God's love. This is absolutely crucial, it seems to me, because - and here I'm back with G.K. Chesterton again - trusting that power has quite simply never been tried.

It astonishes me that people who have found their personal lives changed and renewed by their relationship with God should be so keen to ditch the experience as soon as the crisis is a national one. Solving problems by seizing control never works. Yet we do it again and again, expecting different results.

And what should I do? Well, what I mustn't do is sit around and wait for other people to do the dirty work. It is essential to take the "passive" out of "pacifism" and the only way to stop a thing is to stop it. The first step must be to live a peace-based, nonviolent life myself. That means putting these principles into practice at home, every day, all the time. It also means doing all I can to support projects which explore alternatives to violence and conflict resolution. I believe that peacemaking is a skill. It can be learned.

The world will learn peace in the end. Sadly, I think it may take many hundreds of years, but I am confident that, in the future, nations will use the money once spent on defence to pioneer ways of resolving conflict. It is essential that this happens, because real global change will not take place until it does. We must march; we must agitate; we must argue. We must do everything we can to promote peacemaking as a way. This is not idealism, because it starts with us.

5

My first reading of the Quaker approach to peace was revelatory. It put into words the very position I had arrived at. That was how I wanted to live. I could aspire to such a way of life. In spite of my many subsequent failings, I still try, and have remained as convinced as ever that for me this is the right way. It is not easy. There are many questions for which I have not an easy or ready answer and I have learned to live with the comforts and the discomforts of my conviction. What I do know is that I do not wish to be violent or aggressive towards others, nor do I wish others to act aggressively or violently on my behalf.

My journey came about like this.

During the 1939-45 war I was at school and many of my family and friends were serving in the forces. It soon became apparent that war was not about deeds of valour and the glamour of uniforms. From time to time the commandment I had learnt in childhood, "Thou shalt not kill", would arise in my mind. This was church teaching, yet all the churches I knew at that time seemed in support of war. Somehow "we" were on the side of right. I do remember the powerful recognition that, just as we prayed to God for victory and deliverance, so did the German people; and just as the chaplains on our side blessed the men before battle, so did the other side.

With the ending of the war in Europe came the revelations about the carefully planned and executed extermination of so many people by the Nazi regime. I saw news footage of the death camps recorded as Allied forces advanced. The profound experience of this on a seventeen year old has lived with me ever since, and as I write I feel the same cold horror. Over the following years, many awful aspects of that war were exposed, including the suffering of so many under the Japanese military regime - not to mention the dreadful bombing of Europe by the Allies. The use of the atom bomb which ended the war in the Pacific numbed me, and I still hear my mother's words spoken in response to the accounts of the devastation wrought by the atomic bombs that fell on Nagasaki and Hiroshima: "There will never be another war."

So the years went on. Gradually the church I had grown up with ceased to have relevance. However, its Christian teaching, particularly the second great commandment to love one another, stayed with me. In my early thirties, I found myself on a spiritual search and to my everlasting gratitude was led to Quakers and read the great testimonies. It was, as I have said, as though everything came tumbling into place. The peace testimony cast light on where my experiences and thinking had led me. I was so aware of the sufferings of war. There must be other ways than war of settling differences. There must be other ways of sharing our human experience. I knew then that I could not answer all the questions that arise, such as "What would you do if ...?" and "What about Hitler and his attempt to execute all the Jews, the homosexuals, the mentally ill, the gypsies?" Later, I met a relative who had been a conscientious objector in the 1939-45 war, and he gave me great help. His brother lived in a psychiatric hospital due to injuries received in the 1914-18 war, and indeed died there in the early 1970s. The simplicity of his answer, "I did not want to do to anyone what had been done to my brother," put into words what has remained a truth for me.

I know how frail I am. I know I can react with an immediacy, especially in defence of another. Would I be able to do it with care and with love? I do not know. What I do know is that peace begins in the way I live in relation to all those around me. For me, as for many, there are no big stories to tell of having done anything of great note. I have not been confronted with major situations which demanded of me a really deliberate act of conscience. I constantly ask myself about such matters as the use of my taxes for war purposes. I am a very ordinary citizen, and I live in a society and a world where I am continually reminded of the almost unbelievable inhumanity which we as human beings wreak upon one another. I know that world economics place me in a very privileged position.

At the same time, I am reminded of the loving acts of human beings towards one another and the world in which we live, and I know that we are all one with another. I want to be able to live my life in accord with loving God and my neighbour as myself. In trying to live "in the virtue of that life and power that takes away the occasion of all wars" I know that I have to be constantly vigilant. I know that I frequently find my behaviour wanting. I know that I have no answers to many questions I am asked, nor indeed those I ask myself. Taking a positive position on peace is accepting that I must be active. It is not opting out. It is being in there. It is doing whatever I am capable of doing. It is owning up and saying, "I do not know," and it is saying, "I am engaged in the process."

6

I agree that pacifism may well be an ideal, but I have too many questions. What would I do if I were living in the middle of a conflict zone? What would I do if I had seen my friends and/or family being killed in brutal and unjust circumstances? Or what if I heard of Nazi atrocities and felt that an unstoppable evil was threatening my way of life or existence?

The answer is, of course, that I don't know. I live in a time when I am fortunate not to have to really answer these questions; we do not have conscription; thankfully, we do not have to contemplate a fight for survival of our way of life as many believed in the last two world wars. (Whether they were mistaken in their belief is another debate. Many Quakers and others did not so believe and refused to fight and to take the consequences, becoming social outcasts and victims of the judicial system then in place.)

In another sense too, this is all "too big" for me to use in a practical sense. Yes, I can write letters and attend demonstrations against arms sales and against illegal wars such as the one in Iraq. I can debate the rights and wrongs of pacifism too, but it is unlikely that I will really have to make the decision.

For me it is much more relevant and somehow "do-able" to begin with everyday life and everyday concerns. I can begin with *Advices & Queries*. I can try hard to respond to their questions and provocations in my daily life.

Advice number 31 asks us to "Search out whatever in your own way of life may contain the seeds of war," but for me it is the next Advice, number 32, that really is a help and guide. "Bring into God's light those emotions, attitudes and prejudices in yourself which lie at the root of destructive conflict... In what way are you involved in the work of reconciliation between individuals, groups and nations?"

I think that what I am trying to say is that "peace begins at home", or rather peace begins with you and me. Reading

Advices & Queries, we are repeatedly called on to be thoughtful, questioning, respectful of others and to value others' opinions.

So, what does that mean? Do I live a saintly life, devoid of conflict and malice? Of course not. What it means is that I try in difficult situations to think better of people and their motives than my initial feelings might lead me. I try to be less judgmental; I try to "take a step back" as pop psychology might say. I am successful and unsuccessful to varying degrees. I get angry and have rages and mutter words of criticism and condemnation, *usually to myself*, and I try to avoid using anger and argument to find ways forward.

In my work, I am a union representative and also a school governor. In both contexts there have been, quite recently, controversies and disagreements. At work, there is "restructuring", causing great anxiety and anger for many. I have found myself adopting Quaker principles in meetings: listening to people's comments, questions, feelings, anger, and reflecting back to them a "sense of the meeting" just as we would in our Meetings for Worship for Business. Rather than "going in to battle" I have stuck to debate, argument and persuasion to achieve a fair compromise - involvement and influence in the process.

At the school of which I am governor, a relatively small matter became a great source of conflict and resentment. I remember asking for a period of quiet for us to consider what to do next. We did have some quiet and a way forward was found, where listening to each other was the key, rather than exchanging and repeating firmly held views in the usual adversarial manner.

A further help comes from Advice 17, which asks us whether we "respect that of God in everyone" and ends with the words "Avoid hurtful criticism and provocative language. Do not allow the strength of your convictions to betray you into making statements or allegations that are unfair or untrue. Think it possible that you may be mistaken."

This is what I try to do. Sometimes I fail; sometimes I succeed. For me the working for peace - or pacifism - comes in the trying, and the *keeping* trying.

7

At the first Quaker meeting I ever attended a Friend gave ministry to celebrate the recent abolition of the death penalty. She spoke of the hundred-year struggle by countless Quakers to help bring this about. From that moment I knew I had fallen among friends. For I had long believed that killings by the State through capital punishment were ethically wrong when human justice was so fallible.

That was the mid-1960s, and today I still worship in awe and admiration of those Friends who continue in the struggle to witness to the sanctity of life. For I have now learned what it means, in life-lived terms, for there to be that of God in everyone and that all of life is sacred. I join with those whose vision of life is sacramental, who know that to extinguish a human life or to damage the planet unnecessarily is an act of sacrilege to the whole and to the holiness of life: a diminution of the Spirit.

If I had become a Friend earlier I would also have known

that my call-up for two years' National Service would have confronted me with three stark choices. Friends could serve with the armed forces if they felt the war was just; they might join the Friends Ambulance Unit or other relief work to proclaim the injustice of the war but identify with those suffering it; or they could feel called to take up an absolutist position and face imprisonment for the sake of conscience.

Quakers, having a testimony against all dogma, do not prescribe which of the three choices to make. There is only a compulsion to choose with profound discernment, not a compulsion to pacifism, even if that is deeply ingrained in the texture of the Quaker tradition from its origins. It means, however, that whichever choice is made, the Friend inevitably feels guilty about the other roads not taken. Reconciliation at the end of any international conflict has not always been easy among those who have taken the different paths. It is thought that about a third of the eligible young Friends called up fought in the Second World War, and it was natural that divisions in many Meetings were considerable when they returned, needing long and careful healing.

No one is a pacifist until they have been put to the test, whether in war-time or peace-time. It is a badge that can only be worn after the event. The times are always crying out for those rarest of prophets who can witness powerfully and symbolically to clog up the processes of the war machine and provoke the conscience of the multitude. I have so far failed the test but there is yet time.

Meanwhile, I have been moved to join with the peacemakers. Several of us some years ago initiated Leap

Confronting Conflict, now the lead training organisation within the British Youth Service for conflict resolution and peer group mediation. I have also written songs and musicals and oratorios that told peace stories or celebrated the peaceable way, and I have attempted to live this myself. But I have become too entangled and encumbered to take a pure and clear stand as a pacifist. This needs a less worldly and more spiritual disposition. Quakers at large seem to be in much the same state. As a Society we challenged the immoral and illegal recent war in Iraq only in the ways of the "bourgeois pacifist", courteous demonstrations and polite newspaper letters. The Quaker termites of peace nibbled only imperceptibly at the foundations of power. Our latter-day respectability, economic prudence and lack of youthful vision increasingly hold us back.

As a father, grandfather and Quaker I know what it is to be in that same cleft stick, torn two ways. One, wanting my family to be safe; the other, knowing that all violence begets violence and is a spiritual blasphemy. My heart opposes all war and knows that nuclear war is genocide, an indictable crime against humanity. My head agrees to an armed police force in dire necessity, and to an armed peace-keeping force when aid is being distributed to otherwise starving refugees - both forces needing to be increasingly peace trained. Like others I must live the contradictions and help in the realistic planning of a better world, seeking inspiration to do so from today's occasional prophets of God.

This realism teaches me that it is in the minds of men that neighbourhood disputes begin, which the cornucopia of mediation and conflict resolution skills that Quakers have initiated over 350 years can increasingly address. But it is in the minds of politicians that wars begin and here our techniques and energies need to be of a different order. We give inordinate power to our leaders and must hold it as axiomatic that all power corrupts and absolute power corrupts absolutely.

We see daily in footballer, pop star, multi-national executive, pope and prime minister how the inflation of god-like celebrity and authority corrodes. Only by curbing power through more open, transparent, uncorrupted democratic processes, whether the United Nations or European Union abroad or an elected second chamber and a more forthright Cabinet at home, can we avoid being at the mercy of the psychic sickness that unbridled power induces. Our quest in the twenty-first century is to find new ways of speaking peace to power so that "nation shall not lift up sword against nation, neither shall they learn war any more".

8

I have experienced at first hand less of the effects of war than many people. However, I've seen enough of the effects to convince me that it solves no more problems or eradicates no more evil than it creates. Conflicts have to be solved by negotiation in the end.

In this age, wars can be waged at distance with less risk to the aggressor; trade and commerce operate through global systems and information or disinformation networks are faster and more invasive. More and more commonly can enemies be created to satisfy greed for resources, power or territory, and the people's will for peace is not strong enough to understand or overcome their fear of the enemy, or the perpetrator who may be acting in their name.

I worry about the fact that at the same time we and our children are learning more about war and less about building peace. There is much more information - and indeed entertainment - based on war and the waging of it. The aftermath or the repair of the damage is so often left to the heart-rending, charity-inspiring lesser "film bites" about the consequences. I have never seen a film about the reconstruction of Coventry or Dresden or indeed of Japan after the two nuclear attacks. I suppose it would be less dramatic.

I wholeheartedly support our peace testimony, but on a personal level, although I have feared on a few occasions for my life or the lives of members of my family, I don't know what I would do if I stood with a weapon between them and an attacker. Even if I wanted to, I don't think I would be able to kill or wound - but I have never been tested.

I admire and revere those who dedicate their lives to the cause of peace, sometimes tragically making the ultimate sacrifice. Now I no longer have the courage and strength of my youth, I try to make peace in small ways. I am reminded to "look for ways to mediate" and I also believe in the old slogan: "If you want peace, work for social justice."

9

I was born after the Second World War, but grew up in the shadow of it. My mother is a Russian Jew, and her mother, grandmother and uncle were gassed in a concentration camp. The blight of that horror and my mother's survivor guilt loomed large in my childhood.

One day, as a small child, I watched the news on television - a novelty since we ourselves did not have television - and saw one man shooting another in the head. It was, I think, the first time such a thing had been shown on television (it might have been in the then Belgian Congo) and it caused a furore in the media. It certainly caused a storm in my heart, and the image is with me still. I do not now watch the news on television or violent films; I do not wish to see such images, to become desensitised to the horror, to allow the sanctity of human life to be dulled.

I have not lived through the experience of war, except at a distance, so I cannot say how I would behave if tested. But those childhood experiences made it clear to me both how unthinkable the killing of another human being is, and that the unthinkable happens. It happens daily, all over the world, and we have been responsible for it in recent years in the Falklands, in Afghanistan and in Iraq.

These wars have politicised me, have driven me to go on my first marches for peace, to write letters to my MP, and also to train as a facilitator for the Alternatives to Violence Project, to learn to cope with anger and conflict in my own life, and to enable others to do the same. Anger and conflict are part of the human condition; it is how we deal with them that defines us.

It is not conflict or even anger that is at the root of most violence, I believe, but the notion of "the other". Only by viewing someone as other, less than human, can people torture and kill each other. Such a process led "ordinary" Germans to behave as they did against the Jews, gypsies and homosexuals; it is the beginning of that process, I believe, that allows us to exclude asylum seekers, travellers and some homeless people from our own society, and enables us to ignore the unkindness and violence meted out to members of those communities on a daily basis. It has to stop.

For there is no "other"; we are all one, interconnected.

I cannot imagine killing another human being, and I can't ask someone else to do it for me. It may seem a naïve or simplistic thing to say, but to discuss the issue in a pragmatic way misses the point: it's not a practical matter, but a religious one. It's like entering into a rational argument about whether God exists - it's not a matter of logic, it's on a different plane. A delightful young man of 6 foot 4 (not a Quaker) told me the other day that he had once performed a citizen's arrest. "The other bloke punched me on the nose," he said, "and he didn't believe it when I didn't punch him back, in fact didn't even have my hands up to protect myself. He didn't know what to do."

Pacifism in action: the strongest weapon.

10

I am a pacifist - depending how we define "pacifist"! If it means someone who has never even felt a twinge of temper but is beautifully tranquil and has solved the world's conflicts, well, I have failed. If a pacifist longs for peace, justice and forgiveness, but quarrels, yells, cries and keeps apologising, learns and tries again, then I can count myself a pacifist. As I understand the principle of the Quaker peace testimony, peace is a process where each one of us tries to live a life that shifts the balance towards peace, and therefore towards a just and respectful society. We never give up this divine ideal.

But surely when peaceful means fail, we do have to give up and use force? My observation and my experience tell me violence brings short-term benefits and long-term costs. My father and others of his age were heroes with medals from the Second World War: I admire their courage, loyalty and sense of duty, their willingness to give their lives for others. They also killed and destroyed, and I saw the alcoholism, the scarred and damaged bodies, the orphaned children, the constant grief of the widowed, the fears of the Cold War. Sixty years later, I can still trace the devastating economic effects of that war in too many countries.

I can't sort out Iraq or prevent the next war. The task facing me, as a pacifist, is much smaller: to listen to my three nephews in the army, to understand each one's own ideals and experience and skill and then - but only if it seems right - to offer them a different picture of how problems might be solved. To me, that is what "answering that of God" in them means - not just a heart-to-heart talk, but a soul-to-soul conversation, in which I am as open to change as they are.

I know I have faced the temptation to violence, and I have failed, struggled, learned. No Quaker parents have been perfectly peaceful with their children. I think many have managed not to hit theirs, but all will have been unfair, or sarcastic, or imperfect in some way at some time - of course. I didn't want to be the kind of parent who slapped, but I did not know how to respond more usefully when our children were impossibly, obstinately naughty. I did learn, and years later I know I have been forgiven. I am so proud to see how one is a trained mediator, a good one too, and the other is a trusted childminder. We can change the cycle of violence.

It's the same in the Quaker community. Most of the time the local Friends' meeting really is a loving, supportive, challenging, interesting and enjoyable place to be. Conflict is inevitable among humans, but can we deal with it constructively, or does it destroy us? The traditional Quaker way is to meet in worship, in a small or larger group, where we can trust each other enough to be honest with each other and with ourselves. Whether we know God as a reality, or find richness in a divine myth, I notice that we put aside our egoism. Then we can see the other people involved are people, like us, and peace becomes possible.

Pacifism is not for cowards; it demands the courage to give your life, maybe to live with ridicule, even to break the law. Refusing conscription into the armed forces used to mean being court-martialled or shot. Now, part of my taxes - perhaps half - finances military action and arms sales. I remember the Quaker annual meeting, when more than a thousand considered the request of some of our employees to divert that part of their PAYE tax to peaceful means, such as overseas development. Our *Advices & Queries* remind us: "If you feel impelled by strong conviction to break the law, search your conscience deeply. Ask your meeting for the prayerful support which will give you strength as a right way becomes clear." I could not support such an impractical idea, yet I had the extraordinary experience in that Meeting for Worship of realising that, in order to follow God with our vision for a peaceful world, we had to try. Over the next year, Quakers pushed the matter as far as the European Commission on Human Rights, forcing the question to be considered seriously. This was when I understood the power of an ideal - the power of God.

11

"Force may subdue, but love gains." William Penn, 1692

Isn't the struggle between people spiritual? That is, where the spirit that one person aspires to express is challenged by others living out a different spirit? Are not the outward manifestations of struggle (denial, deceit, challenge, violence, war) just the physical consequences of different dispositions to life? And just as these consequences are written in the histories of our families, communities and nations, do we not sense them in each other? Often we quickly get a sense of the spirit in which another is living from details such as the look in an eye or the way the person holds their body.

I chose to work with difficult adolescents, both to ease their discomfort and the discomfort they caused everyone else. On one occasion one of the girls in my project sent for her boyfriend, whom I had not met before, to beat me up. He came flying up the stairs to where I stood at the top, blocking his way. In three seconds we had come eyeball to eyeball and in an instant he saw no defence in my body, no risk of retaliation, no ill-intent in my eye, no "enemy" to fight in my face, no threat. It was literally disarming.

Though I would not move, he could not hit me. In one sense, there was nothing to hit. From this and other occasions I learned that, when under personal threat, I could put faith in a calm, firm, positive attitude where I didn't have a violent response to hand. Providing I was recognised as another human being (not an enemy, or an object), I was not at risk. A genuine, positive nonviolent disposition can also be an effective defence.

I think our Quaker testimony to peace derives from our sense of how the Spirit calls us to be, in particular how we should approach others and how we should view ourselves. Our denial of war is one specific outcome of this. Quakers have seen that we are all one of another, and have sensed our connectivity at a deep level. We have seen that we are to be equally valued as potential witnesses to the Light, we are each to be equally respected.

So how does the Spirit call us to deal with adversaries, people who are working against our goals, our means, our values or who are threatening us personally? How are we to view conflict, particularly as we are commanded to love our neighbour as (much as) ourselves?

Positively! Conflict derives from our differences, and from these we are shown more of humanity than we can know in ourselves. From our differences we see that our perspective is not the only one, not necessarily the best one, and when combined with others' enables us to see more of Truth than we could see alone. Treating our differences positively, with openness and enquiry, while insisting on our equal right to have our emotions and opinions heard, transforms conflict by influencing our interaction with others.

Conflict also provides the greatest opportunities for personal transformation (as every dramatist knows). Not only do we have to develop understanding, empathy, humour and patience, and to learn to look for common ground and common gain, but we also have to learn to accept and respect our adversaries, however much we reject their behaviour, their views, or their intention.

Yet the Spirit calls for more than this. We are called to live in ways that bring out the very best in each other, that "answer" that of God in us all. When in conflict we would hope that might prompt responses of a different quality, ones that offer both parties openings for growth, reconciliation and forgiveness. Sometimes this is only made possible through our own suffering, where it affirms but resists the oppressor, such as when Gordon Wilson forgave the bombers as his daughter lay in the rubble of the Enniskillen bomb, or when Mandela grew in stature as he provided dignified, positive resistance from his cell in Robben Island.

12

When I first came to Quakers in the mid-1990s, the peace testimony did not trouble me. Gradually, though, the Quaker way changed my life. I started by volunteering overseas with VSO. They sent me to a small Balkan country where I encountered the reality of war and what it does to people.

I arrived in Macedonia just before the Kosovo war began. Soon the population of the town I was living in, a few miles from the Kosovan border, was tripled by refugees. I came to understand how refugees are no different from us, just people caught in the wrong place at the wrong time. I learnt the human cost of violence.

Being so close that I could watch the bombers overhead, I understood the old adage that truth is the first victim of war. While NATO denied using Macedonian airspace, my own eyes told me otherwise. I saw how television shapes images of war. One-off incidents were continually re-shown, giving my panicky parents the impression that I was in danger.

Later, and more positively, I observed the reconstruction effort in Kosovo, and the impact of humanitarian organisations and soldiers acting as peace-keepers. I developed the conviction that civilians have a vital role in peace-building, but they often need to co-operate with the military in the aftermath of violent conflicts.

Unfortunately, this was only the beginning of my hard lessons about violent conflict. In 2001 there was an inter-ethnic armed conflict in Macedonia itself. I was there myself for part of the time. My friends were caught up in it and on both sides. The town I knew was at the centre of it. I experienced shooting, panic, and fear. It was a shock to hear normally rational friends raving with fear and loathing for the other ethnic group. I have witnessed how the approach of war makes people take leave of their senses so that they can come to believe the impossible: that killing and destruction can somehow improve lives, security and human rights.

This experience brought the Quaker peace testimony alive for me. Since then I have been trying to discover what can be done to resolve or, better yet, to prevent violent conflict.

I have found that what I learned in Macedonia and Kosovo was not unique but applies to most wars.

By worshipping often with Quakers I experience unity and equality with others, feeling the connections, the power and the love which exist within and between us. At best we are in touch with a quality of goodness which never leaves us and which counters the despair that human sufferings and failings also always exist. We share one planet and are of one race, the human race. It takes time, and much reflection and study, to hold on to the view that peaceful means must prevail eventually over war as a means of achieving justice.

Gandhi said: "There is no way to peace. Peace is the way." Perhaps those who cannot be pacifists because they think there might be occasions when there is no alternative to war focus too much on those exceptions. If it seems too radical to start with "no war", think about "not this war". Remember the occasions when responding to injustice without violence has worked. In recent years it has brought an end to the division of Europe, apartheid in South Africa, and regimes in the Ukraine and Georgia.

I reject the idea of a "just" war. Wars, by the very nature of the means they use, are never just. They may be fought, at least by some of the protagonists, to right injustice; but that does not make what is done in the war just. People, groups, warlords, nations will join in for their own purposes, while others spur the conflict on from the sidelines by selling arms to both sides.

I feel deeply that using violence to obtain human rights and democracy is a contradiction in terms. Human ends can never justify inhuman means.

My vision is of a world where any state that tried to use aggression against another would be faced by the united resistance of all other governments refusing to sell arms to it; refusing to supply intelligence; and using financial and other sanctions. Instead it would have positive ways to raise its grievances and be heard through international political, economic and legal institutions. Within states, ethnic groups and individuals would also have peaceful ways to raise their grievances because of the universal acceptance of human rights, and access to fair legal systems, officials and police.

Living the Quaker peace testimony is being on the way to peace. I am still on that journey but I am accompanied and supported by Friends in learning about and working out what I can do for peace. I'm not afraid to think about war now. I am more afraid of the consequences if people with concern for others do not face these issues. Can we leave the future of humanity and the planet to leaders who think the ends justify the means, who do not respect all people, or who see life as a struggle against mindlessly evil enemies who deserve to die?

Recommended reading:

Quaker Faith & Practice: The book of Christian discipline of the Yearly Meeting of the Religious Society of Friends (Quakers) in Britain. London: Britain Yearly Meeting, 3rd edition, 2005

Advices & Queries. London: Britain Yearly Meeting, 1994

Ambler, Rex: *Truth of the Heart*. London: Quaker Books, 2001

Chopra, Deepak: *Peace is the Way*. London: Rider, 2005

Curle, Adam: *Another Way*. London: John Carpenter Publishing, 1995

Ellis, George: *Science in Faith and Hope*. London: Quaker Books, 2004

Fisher, Simon: *Spirited Living: Waging Conflict, Building Peace*. London: Quaker Books, 2004

Francis, Diana: *Rethinking War and Peace*. London: Pluto Press Ltd., 2004

Quaker Peace and Social Witness: *Affirming the Light: Ten Stories of Quaker Peace Witness*. London: Quaker Books, 2002

Quaker Peace and Social Witness: *Faithful Deeds: a Rough Guide to the Quaker Peace Testimony*. London: Quaker Books, 2002

Smith, Lyn: *Pacifists in Action*. Sessions of York, 1998

Quaker Quest pamphlets and all of the books listed on the previous page are available from:

The Quaker Bookshop
Friends House, 173-177 Euston Road, London NW1 2BJ
020 7663 1030/31

Or go to www.quaker.org.uk and click on "Publications" and then "The Quaker Bookshop" for a catalogue and on-line shopping.

Some useful websites:

- Conciliation Resources
  www.c-r.org
- Institute of War and Peace Reporting
  www.iwpr.net/home_index_new.html
- International Alert
  www.international-alert.org
- Leap Confronting Conflict
  www.leaplinx.com
- Peace Direct
  www.peacedirect.org
- Peaceworkers UK
  www.peaceworkers.org.uk
- Quaker Peace and Social Witness
  www.quaker.org.uk/peace/index.html
- Responding to Conflict
  www.respond.org